Laurence J. Hyman
Publisher and Creative Director

Laura A. Thorpe
Editor

Laurence J. Hyman
Jim Santore
Art-Direction and Design

David Lilienstein
Distribution Director

Angela Sinicropi
Katy Wilcoxen
Jean Williams
Carolyn Maderious Mann
Editorial Assistants

Jeanne Taggart
Production Assistant

Writers:
Ron Fimrite
Bill Mandel
Bruce Jenkins

Photographers:

Debora Cartwright	Beth Hansen	Robert La Mar
Brad Chaney	Bodie Hyman	Fred Larson
Brad Corbelli	Laurence J. Hyman	David Lilienstein
Dennis Desprois	Michael Jang	Roy Shigley
Roy Garibaldi	Cynthia Kane	Martha Jane Stanton
Stephen Green	Mari Kane	Jon Winet
Otto Greule, Jr.	Tak Kuno	Michael Zagaris

WOODFORD PUBLISHING
4043 23rd Street
San Francisco, CA 94114
415: 824-6610

ISBN: 094262710-5
Library of Congress Catalog Card Number: 89-51939

First Printing: April, 1990

This book was typeset in ITC Berkeley at ProType Graphics of San Rafael, California.
Color separations and sheet-fed printing were done at Mariposa Press, Benicia, California.

Preceding Page: Jellybean artist Peter Rocha commemorates the sweet taste of World Series "Bay's-ball." Photograph by Beth Hansen.

THREE WEEKS IN OCTOBER

Three Weeks in the Life of the Bay Area,
the 1989 World Series, and the Loma Prieta Earthquake

Produced in collaboration with
The San Francisco Giants
The Oakland Athletics
and
Major League Baseball

WOODFORD PUBLISHING
San Francisco

Managers Tony La Russa and Roger Craig get back to business at the start of earthquake-delayed Game 3. Photograph by Michael Zagaris. The San Francisco Ferry Building clock remains frozen for days after the Bay Area's worst earthquake since 1906. Photograph by Laurence Hyman.

PREFACE

The idea for this book of photographs took form as, within a 24-hour period, the two Bay Area Major League baseball teams clinched 1989 pennants. Both ballclubs had enjoyed superb seasons, and fan involvement and community support for the Athletics and Giants ran high. Although the rivalry between the two clubs was traditional and real—with the European press even portraying the Series as a struggle between the "Oakland working class" and the "San Francisco aristocracy"—we all knew the whole Bay Area was already victorious, regardless of the Series outcome.

Our intent was to explore and chronicle the effects of a first-ever Bay Area World Series on the community. Our distinctive geography, architecture, traditions and ambiance would be the focus of the entire world for a brief period; all eyes would be upon us. So, in association with the Athletics and Giants, we decided to turn our cameras on ourselves. We would create a visual record of this rare time, which we assumed would occupy two weeks in October.

We invited a number of talented local photographers to go out and record visual evidence of the community's response to the World Series. We asked three highly-regarded Bay Area journalists to listen to the sounds, smell the smells, and help us remember what this time was like.

Then came the great earthquake of October 17. Only partway into our initial two-week period, the entire Bay Area was suddenly jolted into an unwelcome new world of death, aftershocks, anxiety, rubble, sirens, police cordons, landmarks destroyed, radio and television free (for a time) of advertising, and many people homeless. Long distance phone calls from frightened friends and relatives told us of a distorted world view that the Bay Area had been damaged beyond recognition. We were all reminded of uncertainties of life on not one, but two, major earthquake faults.

Our photographers changed lenses and continued shooting. Our writers now had hard news to report. At once, starting with the sensible good humor of everyone at Candlestick Park that evening, we were all awestruck at how well the entire community responded to the crisis. There was no panic, no stampeding, no looting, no sudden migrations out of town, no accusations. Everyone coped, and helped others do so, and suddenly the community had become truly united and without boundary. The rivalries dissolved. The Bay Area reeled for a day or so, then like a great athlete arose with more energy and vigor than before. Our little book had taken on vast new meaning and historical importance.

Three Weeks in October, as it came to be re-named after the earthquake-delayed World Series extended the framework of our project, is a visual record, an artistic scrapbook, of this unique period in Northern California history.

We wish to thank Pat Gallagher of the Giants and Andy Dolich of the Athletics for their inspiration and assistance, the Front Offices of both ballclubs, Major League Baseball for its cooperation, and the writers and photographers whose work follows.

Laurence J. Hyman
Publisher

December, 1989

The community salutes the first-
ever Bay Area World Series.
Photograph by Beth Hansen.

INTRODUCTION

by Ron Fimrite

Ah, what rarefied air we Bay Area baseball fans breathed that second week in October. Both of our teams, the Athletics and the Giants, would be playing in the World Series, so no matter which of them won, we in this most blessed of all communities would have the world champions. Of course we already had the football champs, the 49ers, but somehow the Series seemed a bigger prize than the Super Bowl, for this time we would not have to share the spotlight with anybody from out of town. No, the baseball title would be decided entirely within our own borders. It was heady stuff, the more so for being such an uncommon occurrence. Only 15 times since the World Series was first played in 1903 had teams from the same metropolitan area fought it out for the championship, and all but two of those intramural Series' had been played in New York. The only non-Gotham matchups had been between Chicago's White Sox and Cubs in 1906 and St. Louis' Cardinals and Browns in 1944. And not since 1956, when the Yankees beat the then-Brooklyn Dodgers had there been a true commuter Series. Granted, the A's and the Dodgers in 1974 and '88 and the Royals and the Cardinals in 1985 had played intrastate Series', but those are not nearly the same. The Giants and Athletics had met in the World Series three times before—but that was decades ago, in 1905, 1911 and 1913. In those days, John McGraw's Giants played in New York's Polo Grounds and Connie Mack managed the Athletics in Philadelphia. Indeed, the metropolitan World Series had become so rare that the once-familiar expression, "Subway Series," had all but fallen into disuse until we revived it in somewhat altered form last October with our localized "BART Series" or "Bay Bridge Series." Best of all, we had achieved these provincial heights before those two teams from down south could stage their own much-publicized, oft-promised but still-unrealized "Freeway Series."

So, as October 14 approached, the whole Bay Area was pretty much swollen with civic pride. Fans of the separate teams were certainly revving up for this showdown, but I think most of us were just happy that both teams had made it this far. The Giants and A's may be opponents on the field, but together they carry the banner of an entire region. In fact, this World Series seemed to us vindication for all those dreary seasons when tut-tutting eastern baseball oracles were proclaiming that the Bay Area was not big enough to support two Major League teams. And there was a time, not that long ago, when even the most optimistic among us had to concede that the experts may have been right. The evidence seemed to be there in the disheartening attendance figures. In the ten years, from 1958 to 1968, that the Giants had the Bay Area and all of Northern California to them-selves, the team prospered, averaging a million-and-a-half fans a year at home, a figure which in those days was considered well above average. But prosperity quickly went 'round the corner for the San Francisco team when that eccentric insurance salesman from Chicago, Charles O. Finley, moved his A's from Kansas City to Oakland in 1968.

For the next ten years, the Giants averaged less than half—736,000 a season—of what they had been draw-ing at home pre-Charlie O. And the A's, despite winning three World Series in succession, didn't do a whole lot better. In only one of those three championship seasons, 1973, did attendance at the Coliseum exceed a million.

And the next year, with yet another title-winner, the home gate actually declined by some 155,000. By 1979, an A's team that was merely a pallid imitation of the great ones earlier in the decade would draw a humiliating 306,763 for the entire season. Critics were calling the Coliseum the Mausoleum. Not that the Giants were luring many fans away from this crypt. In 1974 and '75, they drew only 519,991 and 522,925. You can't print what they were calling Candlestick Park.

The Bay Area was beginning to look like a baseball graveyard. Maybe there wasn't even room here for one ballclub, let alone two. This was a bitter pill for Bay old-timers to swallow, for they could recall the rollicking days of the old Pacific Coast League Oakland Oaks and San Francisco Seals when both Seals Stadium and the Oakland Ballpark would be packed every time the two teams met. Bad baseball towns? How could they say that about an area that had had professional baseball since the 1850s and had spawned such players as Harry Heilmann, Joe Cronin, Joe DiMaggio, Tony Lazzeri, Frankie Crosetti, Lefty Gomez, Jackie Jensen, Frank Robinson and Joe Morgan, to name only a few? It was downright embarrassing. Was it all Finley's fault for flooding the market? Could we blame it on Candlestick? Or were these, oh spare us, really bad baseball towns?

But then came fresh ownership, innovative promotion, better teams and the baseball renaissance of the 1980s, a time when the grand old game once again assumed its preeminent position in the sporting life of the nation. Last season, both teams drew more than two million in home attendance, nearly 4.7 million between them. The Athletics alone attracted 500,000 more fans to the Coliseum in 1989 than they did for all four seasons between 1976 and 1980. Not room enough for two teams, you say? Why, just give us something decent to watch and we'll show up with the best of them. Let's hear no more about bad baseball towns. We may be the smallest of the four two-team markets, but we outdrew Chicago and held our own with New York. And we did it with one ballpark its perennially dissatisfied tenant annually declares a public disgrace.

The World Series, then, would become our showcase. Let viewers across the continent see our ballparks filled to overflowing with demonstrative, knowledgeable, even rabid fans. What the national audience would actually see were two separate species of fan—the appreciative, well-mannered Oakland variety and the noisier, more impassioned sort in San Francisco—and two quite different ballparks—the suddenly prettified Coliseum and ugly old Candlestick, its walls as toughened by the elements as a lighthouse's.

But more than any of this, television watchers would have a chance to see just how impressively beautiful our Bay Area can be in the soft light of Autumn. Indeed, for a brief time in October, our cities would be T.V. stars. And October is, in so many ways, our best month. Just when the rest of the country is starting to bundle up for winter, we are favored with the warm sunshine tourists look for but seldom find in July. What better time, what better place could there be for America's premier sporting event?

That, at least, was the thinking when the Series began. But there would be disappointments. It would be Candlestick-cold in the Coliseum for those first two night Series games. And the games themselves would be one-sided bores. Not until the Series moved across the Bay to San Francisco for Game 3 were we permitted an opportunity to show off unashamedly. What a brilliant day was October 17, warm, clear and bright. Illuminated by twilight even Candlestick Park, at five o'clock, looked beautiful. And views from the omnipresent Goodyear Blimp gave testimony to the Bay's bountiful charms. This was baseball weather at its best. See, we could say to the rest of the world, this is where the World Series should be played every year.

It would not be long before we would be sending out a somewhat different message. But at the end of those three weeks in October we would still have cause to salute ourselves. Not for our baseball this time. Not for our weather. Not even for our beauty. No, this time we would show the world something of our courage, our fortitude and our resiliency. And when you come right down to it, that's a much more important message.

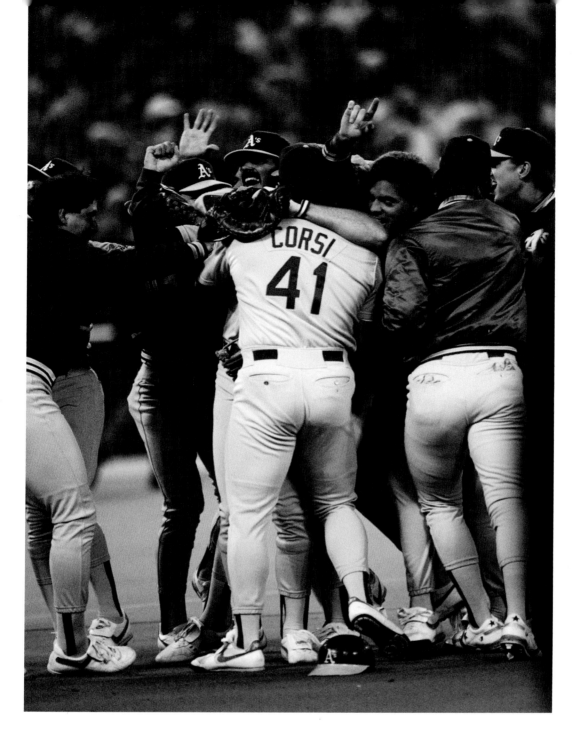

The A's rejoice after winning the pennant in Toronto. Mark McGwire sprays champagne in the clubhouse, while Rickey Henderson shares a moment with his delighted mother. Photographs by Michael Zagaris.

Seconds after closing down the Chicago Cubs in the last game of the National League playoffs, pitcher Steve Bedrosian is embraced by Terry Kennedy and Matt Williams. The ecstatic Giants revel in their first pennant in 27 years. Photographs by Stephen Green.

After capturing the pennant, Mike Krukow lets his emotions flow, Giants owner Bob Lurie and NLCS MVP Will Clark congratulate one another, and Robby Thompson meets with the media. Photographs by Martha Jane Stanton.

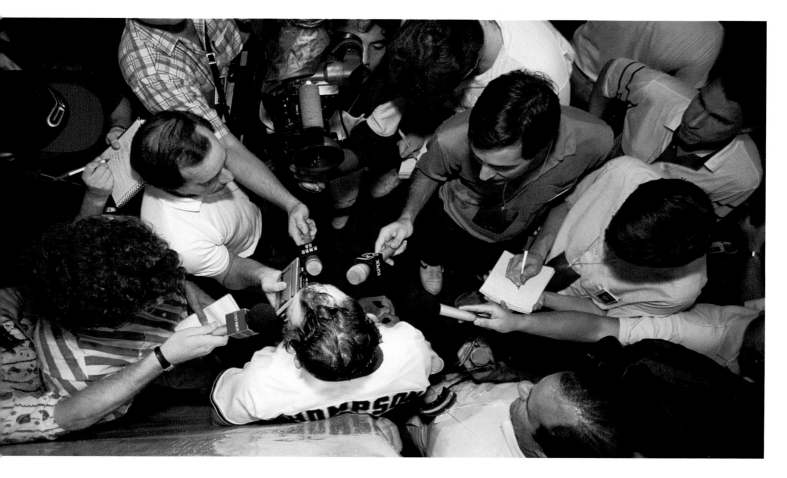

THREE WEEKS IN OCTOBER

by Bill Mandel

Years slip by and we hardly notice. Kids grow up. School opens and closes and opens again. Christmas swings 'round so often you'd swear someone scheduled it every six months. And then, suddenly, comes a short span of time so explosively rich, so filled with vivid touches of the unique—be it joy, triumph, terror or disaster—that it stays with us always, and we remember it later moment-by-moment, as if it went on forever. It is a time when time stands still.

The heart of October 1989 was such a time in the life of the Bay Area. Always a golden month in Northern California, October 1989 began sweeter than usual because the Oakland Athletics and the San Francisco Giants had battled their way triumphantly across the long, hot baseball summer, to win pennants in the American and National Leagues. As the rest of the nation stood by, a local dream would come true: The Bay Area would have the World Series, the Fall Classic, the central legend of the national pastime, all to itself. "The Battle of the Bay," "The BART Series," "The Bay Bridge Series," "Bay's Ball," the headline writers called it.

After enough cross-city hype to inflate 100 Goodyear blimps, the Series finally began. The A's stylishly won the first two games at their Coliseum and the action shifted eight miles west, to infamous, much-maligned Candlestick Park. And then, at the now-famous stroke of 5:04 p.m. on Tuesday, October 17, as a world-wide television audience turned its eyes toward Candlestick in anticipation of Game 3, history trembled. The earth quaked.

Twelve miles beneath Loma Prieta Mountain in the hills near Santa Cruz, the San Andreas fault slipped. In a moment, a slab of earth 11 miles deep by 22 miles long had been thrust more than four feet upward and nearly six feet to the north with a force later rated at 7.1 on the Richter scale. The energy released during the 15 seconds of the Loma Prieta quake was 10 times greater than all the bombs used in World War II, including the two Big Ones that ended it.

The tremors rolling along the fault would collapse a section of the Bay Bridge, bring down the two-tiered Cypress structure of Interstate 880 in Oakland, devastate those portions of San Francisco's Marina District that had been built on landfill, kick the legs out from under old buildings South of Market, heavily damage downtown Santa Cruz, send houses tumbling down hillsides in the Santa Cruz mountains and destroy the oldest sections of Watsonville. Sixty-five people would die; 439 would be hospitalized; 2,874 of the injured would be treated at hospitals and released; nearly 5,000 people would be left homeless. The cost of repairing earthquake damage would be set at $10 billion—that's 10,000 million dollars.

At the same time, the October 17 earthquake would offer Northern California a chance to ennoble itself with good and selfless works as the world watched. To its eternal credit, Northern California grasped that chance and ran with it. Early heroes appeared like a sudden rain to seek survivors in the collapsed Cypress structure and help the wounded from their crippled homes in the Marina. Others stood in the darkened streets and directed traffic. Police officers and firefighters worked 24-hour shifts to protect the public. Restaurant owners gave out free food. Open hearts pumped money, clothing, bedding. Corporations dug deep for millions in earthquake-relief contributions. Volunteers continued to help the displaced weeks after the earthquake's novelty faded.

For a moment, and just a moment, the Bay Bridge World Series was pushed aside. Saying, "Baseball does not want to intrude. We know our place, and our place is to wait until it is appropriate (to resume the Series)," Baseball Commissioner Fay Vincent postponed Game 3 first for a week and then for another three days. The players tried to hold their edge. Some, like Will Clark of the Giants and Dave Parker of the A's, complained about the layoff. Clark said he longed for his hunting dog and the marshes of Louisiana. Parker, even more blunt, said, "I don't live around here anyway." Others, such as Dave Stewart of the A's and Matt Williams of the Giants, showed their mettle by pitching in to help their communities, visiting shelters for quake victims in Oakland and San Francisco.

Exactly 10 days after the Loma Prieta quake put time on hold, 62,000 people were back at Candlestick for Game 3, although it was obvious that a lot of the fans were having some difficulty getting re-involved in baseball after the upheavals of the previous week and a half. And then, three batters into the first inning, Giants pitcher Scott Garrelts came barber-close to A's slugger Jose Canseco with a sizzling fastball and Canseco took fist-clinching exception. Now the crowd really roared. Baseball was back. The clock of time ticked on.

In an October people would remember all their lives, there had been no real losers and more than one winner. As Giants fan Charlie Passalcqua told a reporter after Game 1, "The Bay Area has already won it. This is just to decide where they're going to hold the parade."

On Sunday, October 8, the A's captured the American League pennant, and on the following afternoon the Giants became the National League champions. Three weeks later, on Saturday, October 28, the last game of the World Series was played. Three weeks. It all happened in just three weeks.

*   *   *

The Giants and the A's both had something to prove coming into the Bay Bridge World Series. The A's needed to live down the humiliation of 1988, when the American League champions, sporting the best record in baseball, lost in five horrifying games to a Los Angeles Dodgers club so hobbled that the Series hero — Kirk Gibson — nearly needed a walker to complete his home run trot. The Giants, still angry over blowing the National League Championship Series to the St. Louis Cardinals in 1987, were eager to show the pundits just how wrong they'd been in picking the Giants to finish no better than third or fourth in the National League West. It had been 27 years since the Giants had appeared in a World Series, 35 years since they'd won.

The A's, again the owners of the best regular-season record, completed their five-game rout of the Toronto Blue Jays in the American League Championship Series on Sunday, October 8, in Toronto's SkyDome. It was a playoff marked by Rickey Henderson's dominating attitude on the bases, Jose Canseco's space-shot home run and mustachioed reliever Dennis Eckersley shooting strikeout victims with an imaginary six-gun.

In an equally dominating manner, the Giants finished off a five-game defeat of the Chicago Cubs at Candlestick the next day. Will Clark's bat ruled the National League Championship Series right through the eighth inning of Game 5, when Clark rolled a two-run, pennant-winning single up the middle against Cubs reliever Mitch "Wild Thing" Williams as 62,000 fans went hoarse.

The A's were in. The Giants were in. It was to be a hometown World Series.

The *Examiner's* Burr Snider wrote: "Chicago's a brawny, bluesy kick in the butt, and Mondo Toronto is chrome-dome shiny and slicker than owl spit, but come on, folks, the World Series ended up right where it's supposed to be: Here. Home. Bayside. Heaven. They don't like us out there, people. And you know what? They shouldn't. We got it all, just like Bogie and Bacall. And now we got the champs, too. How can we lose?"

After the Giants clinched, there were five fallow days before the Bay Bridge Series was to begin. They were five days of growing excitement and cross-Bay boasting magnified enormously by the presence of network television. The Bay Area had been transformed temporarily into New York City. This was different from 1984's Democratic National Convention, when San Francisco was briefly the national news focus. Then, Washington brought its politicians and New York its media hordes to San Francisco to watch themselves from a slightly different perspective. As the World Series loomed, the Bay Area itself was being projected on a national scale. Not only were Kevin Mitchell and Mark McGwire big shots in Northern California, they were big shots wherever people watched TV. Living close to this, we sometimes forgot it. Which is why some Bay Area viewers were surprised when Billy Crystal went on David Letterman the week before the Series and did a Will Clark impression. Hey, how does he know about The Nooshler (Clark's famous game face)?

Mayor Art Agnos of San Francisco and Mayor Lionel Wilson of Oakland filled the five-day wait getting on each other's nerves. Agnos declined to make the usual mayor-to-mayor wager on major sports events, saying Oakland had nothing he particularly wanted in the way of stakes. Wilson fired back that Agnos might need a large marble statue of a foot implanted firmly in his mouth. The two made up with an abrazzo on "The CBS Morning News."

Left to stew five days, the media naturally fermented. The weekend the Series opened, the *Sunday Examiner & Chronicle* presented an overheated point-counterpoint debate between a temporarily unhinged partisan of the Giants and an A's fan.

"My problem with the A's," I wrote, "runs deeper than San Francisco vs. Oakland, National League vs. American League, designated hitter vs. baseball, softball uniforms vs. Major League uniforms. The major contrast between the Giants and the A's is tradition vs. modernity, hope vs. cynicism, confidence vs. bragging. In sum, the way we think things used to be vs. the way we know things are. If the A's made a movie, we could call it 'Outlaw Biker Ballplayers from Hell.' The Giants are 'Rocky.' "

Fired back *Examiner* reporter Scott Winokur: "The A's, like Oakland itself, are authentic. They've paid their dues and earned their day in the sun. Give it to them now. They deserve this final victory. Oakland and the East Bay need it. There's a great deal that's good in Oakland, but it's a constant struggle—with drugs, with traffic, with public education. Oakland isn't pretentious. It isn't gazing in the mirror saying, 'Aren't I wonderful?' San Francisco's going to do that one of these years and find out it's got a lot in common with Dorian Gray."

Once the A's and Giants entered the postseason in the first week of October, the local papers were filled with little else. The usual news fixations—crime, drugs, the homeless, AIDS—were pushed rudely aside. The 1989 World Series, it turned out, was in news terms the exact opposite of Christmas. The haves feel guilty for their abundance at Yuletide. Media parades of other people's problems soothe their consciences. There was none of that in early October, as baseball headed for the big finale. Sympathy then went not to those without enough to eat but to Candy Maldonado, he of the upper-six-figure income, for not having enough to hit.

Why the seeming indifference to reality? Because baseball is very important to many people but it doesn't really matter. It is connected in no way to reality. Naturally, we're eager to be swept away on its tsunami of make-believe. Why can't we make it 40 games out of 70?

As Game 1 approached, local baseball fervor drove ticket prices beyond nosebleed levels. "It's off the wall, the biggest World Series I've seen," said Stephen Cucci of Premier Tickets in San Francisco. Ticket brokers were asking, and getting, $750 for good seats at the Coliseum and Candlestick Park, $200 just to get inside. In Pebble Beach, Michael and Pam Smith accidentally tossed their World Series tickets into the trash just before it was collected. They followed the garbage truck to the dump and spent two hours diving through refuse to get their tickets back.

The fervor was not geographically confined. Some households found their tying binds stretched to the breaking point as the Bay Bridge Series approached. One such was another, though unrelated, Smith clan, this one composed of Bill and Sarah, of San Francisco. They saw political events sufficiently eye-to-eye to march together in a pro-choice rally in San Francisco on the Series' opening weekend. Then they parted company to watch the games on separate TVs in separate houses.

"I can't understand why she thinks the A's should win the Series," Bill Smith said. "The Giants are twice as good, they have three times as much local tradition. And she was born in San Francisco, for God's sake."

Firing right back, Sarah Smith said, "He is such a fool on this issue. He doesn't understand. I love (A's catcher) Terry Steinbach. He almost stopped talking to me after I told him that. And he walks out of the house when I cheer for Rickey."

*　　　　　*　　　　　*

Game 1 began at 5:24 p.m. on Saturday, October 14. The A's won 5-0. Dave Stewart shut out the Giants. A day later, the A's won Game 2, 5-1. Mike Moore shut down the Giants. Just before Game 1, Mayors Wilson and Agnos jointly unveiled a $2,000 trophy shaped like the Bay Bridge that would go to the winning team. "These two teams," Wilson said, "are like brothers and sisters."

*　　　　　*　　　　　*

It was hot, still and sunny on the afternoon of Tuesday, October 17. Quite a few fans filing into Candlestick Park for Game 3 made jokes about "earthquake weather." Few realized that the temperature at 5:00 p.m. was 81 degrees, same as the high on April 18, 1906.

The first thing people at Candlestick noticed at 5:04 p.m. was a roar. Maybe a jet from nearby San Francisco International Airport had swooped too low over the stadium. Then vibration began, as if fans in the upper deck had decided, en masse, to stamp their feet. Nanoseconds later, the supposedly solid concrete floor of the 29-year-old structure started to roll like ocean waves and kept rolling for 15 seconds. It seemed much longer. Glass in the luxury boxes that hang from the upper deck rattled. The light towers swayed dizzily. People were frozen in panic-born, tunnel vision eye-lock. A few yelled out, "Earthquake!"

When the underfoot mambo finally stopped, a huge cheer arose. Most Californians had been through quakes before, though none quite like this. Except for a few chunks of concrete that flew away from expansion joints in the upper deck, as planned, Candlestick had remained solid, although fans would not know until later that the park had finished receiving a $28 million seismic-safety upgrade less than a year earlier. The shared expectation was that the game would proceed, if only the lights and the scoreboard would come back on. A guy sitting near me turned and said, "Great. The networks are going to give us more grief for this than they did for Sister Boom Boom."

ABC, the network covering the World Series, was in no condition to give anyone grief at that moment. At 5:04, ABC announcer Tim McCarver was describing taped highlights of Game 2 as part of the pre-game show. When the broadcast booth started shaking, McCarver joked, "I didn't know Parker hit the ball THAT hard." "This has got to be the greatest opening in the history of TV," cracked play-by-play announcer Al Michaels before fully realizing the magnitude of what was happening. ABC was then knocked off the air, as millions of television screens across the country turned to tweed video static.

KNBR radio announcer Hank Greenwald, the voice of the Giants, was pretty smooth under pressure. Hearing that the quake had been given an immediate Richter rating of 6.9, he quipped, "Yeah, but the East German judge only gave it a 6.2."

Across the Bay at 5:04, time and obsolete engineering were catching up to the Bay Bridge and to 1.5 miles of the double-decked Cypress structure of Interstate 880 in Oakland. On the non-suspension part of the bridge east of Treasure Island, a section of the roadway on the upper deck of the bridge pulled free and fell to the lower, cutting a hole straight through. Air and the Bay below were visible through the hole.

Bruce Stephan, an engineer from San Francisco, was returning home on the upper deck of the bridge when the roadway collapsed. As he later recounted his experience, his car started to jump up and down as the 5:04 tremors hit. Then the road beneath him gave way, throwing him to the lower deck and nearly through it into the Bay. "We were falling through the bridge, and there was nothing to catch us. I turned to (his co-worker) Janice and said, 'We're going to die.' " Then a twisted piece of the bridge caught the car and held it suspended over the water. Stephan climbed out his window and dragged his dazed and bleeding co-worker to safety. "This is my second life," Stephan said, "because I died back there."

Thomas Stevens, an eyewitness to the I-880 freeway collapse, told the *Chronicle*:

"It was like a big, giant, long ocean wave, and behind each wave a portion of the freeway collapsed. I just started crying. There was nothing I could do. Then I started thinking of all those people who'd been driving on the freeway and I said, 'Please God, let that freeway hold.' But I knew it wouldn't hold."

Volunteers who live in the West Oakland neighborhood ran immediately to the pancaked freeway, trying to help those screaming for assistance by piling their bodies one on top of another so rescuers could climb 30 feet up to the elevated roadway. Wrote the *Examiner's* Stephanie Salter: "Months or years from now, when we once again find ourselves doubting the basic goodness that lies in the human soul, the instinctive courage that simmers unseen in the common man and woman, we must remember that fallen highway and the human ladder pressed against it."

Early estimates put Cypress structure fatalities at 250 or more, but that figure was later reduced to 41, including one man whose crushed Volvo carried the bumper sticker, "Nature bats last." Authorities said the death toll would have been much higher if it hadn't been for the World Series. Some people who would normally have been on the Cypress at 5:04 p.m. were at Candlestick Park, while others had gone home early to catch the game on television.

In San Francisco's Marina District, expensive homes and apartment houses built on what had once been a bayfront lagoon sagged to the ground, as if detonated from within by dynamite. At 1842 Jefferson Street, Dianne Featherston, a nurse, and her husband, Keith, were just settling in to watch the World Series on television.

"Everything was falling down, everything was coming off the wall," Dianne Featherston later recalled. "The building started to collapse. We knew we had to get out of there fast. I got outside and saw buildings falling to the ground up and down the street. I went over to help, even though I didn't have anything to work with. The first woman I got to in a building at Scott and North Point had a broken hip. I just made sure she didn't move and waited for help to come.

"Young paramedics came running to the neighborhood, seemingly out of nowhere. You could hear people screaming from under the wreckage of a building at Divisadero and North Point. Heroes rushed in, real heroes, and started pulling floorboards up, going through the rubble trying to reach the trapped ones and pull them to safety."

The crowd at Candlestick had no way of knowing that this was more than a scary shake. Then fans who had brought radios to the game started hearing hard-to-believe reports that the Bay Bridge had collapsed, that the Marina was in flames, that a freeway had fallen in Oakland. Word spread.

When the tremors stopped, the players left their dugouts and stood on the field. They motioned to their families to come down from the stands and join them.

"It was unbelievable," said Giants pitcher Mike Krukow. "When nature wants to make a point, it sure puts things in perspective pretty quick. I was on the field and you could see the backstop moving a good 15 feet. I don't know what it was like in the stands, but it almost knocked us down on the field."

Jose Canseco said, "At first I thought it was one of my migraine (headaches) coming on. But it was just an earthquake."

A's equipment manager Frank Ciensczyk: "Stan Javier's eyes went wide open. Once it was over, players were saying, 'So that was the big one.' And then they couldn't stop talking about it."

Most of the A's players, still in uniform, climbed into the team bus and began a 2-1/2 hour ride back to Oakland. Others had brought their cars to Candlestick. Tony Phillips was riding with Lance Blankenship. The momentarily rattled Phillips told Blankenship to choose whatever route he wished back to Oakland, "But one thing: I ain't going over no bridges."

Canseco and his wife, Esther, got into their Porsche and drove away. A newspaper photographer later caught Canseco sitting in the passenger seat, in uniform, while leather-dressed Esther pumped gas.

Forty minutes after the quake, when it became apparent that power was out all over the area, Commissioner Fay Vincent suspended Game 3 until at least the next day. Candlestick Park's public address system went down with the scoreboard and the lights, so a black-and-white San Francisco police car drove over the turf, parked behind home plate and lent its battery-powered bullhorn to the public address announcer, who asked everyone to go home. Fans leaving the park were able to see a tall column of smoke rising from the Marina. In the gathering dusk, they noticed that the highrises of downtown stood dark. When they turned on their car radios, they started to understand the gravity of what had happened.

*   *   *

Recovery began at dawn on Wednesday, October 18. It soon became clear that the *Chronicle's* big, black headline–"HUNDREDS DEAD IN HUGE QUAKE"–was slightly exaggerated. There were proud memories of the night before, when strangers helped strangers and few urban blackout nightmares came true. San Francisco, said the *Examiner,* was "a city triumphant." There was one problem, though: The national media were obsessed with the quake and wouldn't leave it alone. People around the country thought oft-televised scenes of destruction in the Marina, on the Bay Bridge and the Cypress structure were typical of widespread damage that, in fact, did not exist.

Wrote Rob Morse of the *Examiner:* "The national news has painted San Francisco as completely devastated by the earthquake. Dan Rather stood in front of the cameras with a three-day growth of beard and a fatigue jacket, as if he'd just crawled out of the Cypress structure behind him (instead of just stepping from his limousine with its bowl of fresh fruit). The burning block in the Marina, the collapsed homes in the Marina and the ruined Cypress structure have been shot enough times from enough angles so that everyone's out-of-town relatives have been hysterical."

It became symbolically important to show the world that the Bay Area was running again. For this, it eventually became clear, nothing would be better than an early resumption of the World Series.

The day after the quake, Commissioner Vincent met with Giants and A's officials and then held a press conference at the powerless St. Francis Hotel that was lit by hundreds of candles burning in silver candelabras.

"Cancelling the World Series is a major step I'm not prepared to do," Vincent said. "However, it has become very clear to us in Major League Baseball that our concern, our issue, is really a modest one. With the search for victims still going on, with this community still reeling from a disaster, a decision was made not to play baseball before Tuesday (a week after the quake)."

Oakland Mayor Wilson agreed, saying, "I felt it would be inappropriate to play baseball in our city while there were bodies resting under that concrete (on I-880)."

San Francisco Mayor Agnos, who right after the quake brushed aside questions about the World Series as "not a priority right now," later convinced Vincent to postpone resumption of Game 3 a few more days to Friday, October 27. With the Bay Bridge and key freeways out of commission, Agnos said, residents needed extra time to establish travel patterns before baseball resumed.

The weekend following the earthquake was enlivened – and the argument for looking forward underscored – by the discovery in the Cypress ruins of Buck Helm, a 57-year-old longshoreman who'd miraculously survived in the rubble for 89 hours in his crushed Chevy Sprint. After another two hours of feverish work, rescuers took the still-conscious Helm from his car amidst cheers and tears from their bone-tired colleagues.

Helm immediately became grist for the earthquake myth mill. "Buck Helm was just too tough to die," began the *Examiner's* ode, prematurely. Helm died of his injuries on November 19. At the time, however, his survival was widely accepted as a much-needed symbol of rebirth and recovery. The waitress who served him cherry pie in rural Weaverville, where his children live, was quoted as saying, "He's ornery. He's tough as nails." Representatives of telemovie producers immediately descended on the Helm family.

On Monday, six days after, following a weekend of upbeat news centered on Helm's discovery, Agnos felt San Francisco was ready. "Emotionally, the people of San Francisco are resilient," Agnos told a press conference where the issue of "appropriateness" kept coming up. "They've shown in their response to this crisis they're made of the right stuff. At some point life goes on and comes back to where it was before. That doesn't mean you forget the people who were hurt or lost, but there's room to continue life. Anyone who thinks San Francisco can't cope with the resumption of the World Series and everyday life underestimates the strength of this city."

The well-educated Vincent added, "Churchill did not close the cinema houses in London during the blitz. It's important for life to carry on to show that San Francisco is not wounded."

However, even some of the players wondered if the baseball spirit was still there. In an attempt to loosen his team up, A's Manager Tony La Russa flew his players to Phoenix, site of the A's spring training camp, for two days of pre-Series workouts in the sun.

"We showed up in Phoenix and there were all these people in the stands," La Russa reported. "That really touched me. It's like somebody was saying, 'Baseball is great. Baseball means something.' When the day was over, I felt this tugging," he said, pointing to his heart. "I had some positive vibes, but then I had another tug. A different kind. I was embarrassed. I mean, aren't we supposed to feel guilty? It confused the hell out of me. When I drive by 880, I feel a lot of emotion. Then about 10 miles down the road I'm getting all full of myself, full of the team. And I start feeling guilty again."

La Russa said he would tell his team before Game 3, "Be honest. If you feel good, you deserve to feel good. They're calling this the forgotten World Series, but if you play well in this situation, it will have more meaning than any World Series that has come before. Nobody's ever been asked to do this."

Giants Manager Roger Craig, who led his team on a visit to a relief shelter after the quake, now took the long view: "They'll be playing baseball long after they stop burying and grieving for the dead."

Public opinion sampled by the California Poll showed that 83 percent of Northern Californians wanted the Series to resume while 12 percent preferred cancellation. A similar survey in Southern California turned up an approval rating of just 75 percent, revealing that some Southern Californians just can't stand the idea of a Northern California team winning the World Series.

Bay's ball, the everybody-wins, don't-really-root idea of pan-Bay Area happiness over the World Series was fairly popular before the earthquake, although some fans insisted that the presence of two big league franchises in the same market is bound to give rise to a scintilla of partisanship. In other words, regional patriotism aside, they still reserved the right to scream "A's are No. 1!" and "Go Giants!" as they wished. Team identification, however, seemed even smaller-minded after the quake, when people were supposedly happy just to be alive and housed.

A resumption date of Friday, October 27 was set. A few days before that, *Chronicle* columnist Herb Caen suggested that fans be handed the lyrics to "San Francisco" as they entered Candlestick. "San Francisco," a rousing, hokey number written for the 1936 musical of the same name, is really about America coming back from the Depression of the 1930s. Giants management took Caen's suggestion and added a few fillips of its own: People would be asked to shake hands with those around them, and the ceremonial first ball, originally scheduled to be thrown out by Giants immortal Willie Mays, would be thrown out by 12 heroes of the earthquake — firefighters, police officers, utility workers, doctors, Red Cross volunteers and private citizens who risked their lives to prove a point: The worst brought out the best in the Bay Area.

Friday, October 27 was also sunny and warm. The thousands filing back into Candlestick Park for the resumption of the World Series were a bit tentative. Ticket takers tore the small rain checks from tickets that fans had saved from the 17th. "Earthquake checks," one ticket taker kept saying with a smile. You could see fans walking a little gingerly, testing the hard concrete beneath their feet. Before the game, they traded war stories about where they'd been and where they'd gone after the quake. Arms were upraised to point out the swaying light towers and the rattling luxury box glass. An announcement that the public address system was now backed up by a diesel generator drew appreciative applause and laughter. There were a lot of comments of the, "Now where were we when we were so rudely interrupted?" variety. A thin atmosphere of celebration overlay a deeper sense of unease that, for millions in the Bay Area, would not recede for months, if ever.

*   *   *

The A's won Friday night's Game 3, 13-7. Dave Stewart mercilessly shut down the Giants. The A's won Game 4, and the World Series, on Saturday night, 9-6, as Mike Moore baffled the Giants until the sixth inning. That game was marked by the Giants' only outburst of the Series, a spirited six-run rally spread over the sixth and seventh innings. Until that rally, Giants fans had been spared suffering. Like the Giants players, they were numb. They had made peace with their fate. That rally woke them up, broke their hearts one more time and reminded them how much it really hurts to lose.

After the game, Giants General Manager Al Rosen, a former American League Most Valuable Player and a man who lives to win, went through the A's clubhouse congratulating the men who'd just thrashed his team. Meanwhile, A's star Rickey Henderson, the reputed hot dog, was in the Giants' clubhouse giving his erstwhile opponents hugs. Bay's ball indeed.

Out of respect for the dead, there was no champagne in the A's clubhouse as they celebrated victory in the 86th and longest World Series. (The previous record for longevity was held by the 1911 Series that was postponed by rain for nearly a week. Its participants: The New York Giants and the Philadelphia Athletics.) Dennis Eckersley spoke for many of his teammates when he said, "I'm happy, but I feel kind of guilty for being happy. But it took me 15 years to do this, so I'm going to enjoy it."

Spirits were much more ebullient two days later, on Monday, October 30, when the A's arrived at Jack London Square in Oakland by ferry boat from Alameda for a victory rally.

Three thousand fans cheered and waved brooms to symbolize the A's sweep of the Giants. "You're looking at the best team in the world," said first baseman Mark McGwire.

"Oakland has this image as the Bay Area's second city," Peter Berzins, an Alameda sales represenative told the *Chronicle*. "Well, we have the world's best baseball team."

Pitcher Dave Stewart, Oakland native and World Series Most Valuable Player, hoisted the championship trophy and told the crowd, "We want to show you what belongs to all of us," and added, "I want to say from the bottom of my heart that, to me, Oakland and the Oakland A's have one thing in common: The cream always rises to the top."

Rickey Henderson said: "No. 1, huh? This is probably one of the greatest moments of my career. I'm so happy that the Oakland A's gave me a chance to come back to Oakland."

Listening to all of this with a smile was Sister Mary Magdalene, an administrator at Dave Stewart's alma mater, St. Elizabeth's High School. "This," she said, "helps us get back to reality."

*   *   *

They held a memorial service for the I-880 dead in Oakland's West of Cypress neighborhood the day after the A's swept the World Series. Another purpose of the gathering was to salute members of the community who ran to the collapsed Cypress structure the evening of October 17 to dig with their hands, looking for survivors. The site of the meeting was Liberty Hall, a Victorian building erected in 1877 that has now survived two substantial earthquakes. It is the new home for various community services in the West of Cypress area.

Fred Ferguson, director of Liberty Hall, told 300 people, "The actions of those who helped without thought of their own safety demonstrated a sense of power that lets you know that people are capable of doing anything if they allow that positive spirit, that strength that comes with knowing that God's power and people power can do and take care of anything."

A short distance away, Dave Stewart was telling a TV interviewer, "As I said before the Series, if we should win or the Giants should win, it's the Bay Area that's the real winner."

That Sunday, the *Examiner* ran an unsigned editorial written by Warren Hinckle. What Hinckle wrote about San Francisco applies just as well to the entire Bay Area. The editorial said, in part:

"Each time San Francisco was destroyed, it was rebuilt for the better. The coals of destruction never cooled before the vision of a better city took flame. The unique character of this Queen City of the Pacific and the bravery of its men and women forged the soul of a city that has never learned how to die.

"This earthquake has brought San Franciscans together in a spirit of self-help and innovation as has no event since 1906. The world's favorite city now has that which is said to be impossible in American lives — a second act."

All this, and much more, happened during three weeks in October, 1989.

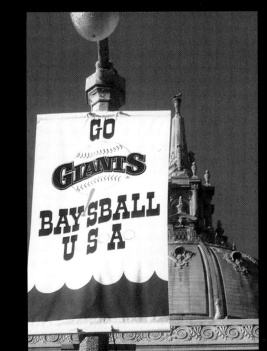

The sun sets over an expectant Bay Area that has long awaited a World Series matchup between the two local teams. Photograph by Roy Shigley. Both cities display their enthusiasm prominently. Photographs by (left) Jon Winet and (right) Otto Greule, Jr./Allsport USA.

Fans remain loyal to their teams, for better or for worse. Photograph (left) by Michael Jang. All other photographs by Beth Hansen.

Local merchants find ways to mix business with pleasure, as fans of all ages wait expectantly for the Series to begin. Photograph by Michael Jang. Photograph (top) by Beth Hansen.

Most of the people at a pre-Series rally outside the Oakland Coliseum are staunch A's followers, but some fans refuse to take sides in the Battle of the Bay. Photographs by Beth Hansen.

A pre-Series rally solicits support for Prop P, the Ballpark Initiative, as well as for the Giants. Photographs by Roy Shigley.

The Giants' success is evident from City Hall to the financial district to neighborhood businesses. Photographs by (L-R) Beth Hansen, Michael Jang, Beth Hansen.

Students at Bret Harte Elementary School rate their team #1. Photograph by Jon Winet. Co-workers agree to disagree about the outcome of the Series. Photograph by Michael Jang.

A doorman at San Francisco's St. Francis Hotel welcomes visitors to Giants territory. Photograph by Michael Jang. Bay Area baseball fans mix and match their loyalties. Photograph by Beth Hansen.

31

On the preceding page, Oakland's Lake Merritt. Photograph by Roy Shigley. Balloons herald a Series kick-off party at the Oakland Museum, which also schedules a special baseball exhibit, "Diamonds Are Forever." Photographs by Beth Hansen.

Dual allegiances are celebrated
in the most unlikely places.
Photograph by Brad Chaney. A
full moon hangs over San Francisco's Russian Hill. Photograph
by Beth Hansen.

A Giants fan kayaks at Ocean Beach. Photograph by Michael Jang. The A's loyal following includes the very young and the not-so-young. Photographs by Beth Hansen.

Bay Area Rapid Transit links the
East Bay to San Francisco.
Photograph by Roy Shigley. Thousands utilize BART to attend games
in Oakland. Opposite page, desper-
ate fans try their luck among the
more fortunate. Photographs by
Beth Hansen.

The A's band performs as the Coliseum parking lot fills before Game 1. Photographs by Michael Jang.

A Giants fan displays top drawer enthusiasm. Photograph by Michael Jang. Coliseum groundskeepers apply post-season finery to the field as players work out. Photograph by Brad Corbelli.

Peculiar sights seem to be the
rule rather than the exception
during the World Series. Photographs by (top) Brad Corbelli
and (bottom) Bodie Hyman.

Supporters of both teams find their loyalties are – at the very least – skin deep. Photographs by Michael Zagaris. Injured Giants pitcher Dave Dravecky discovers many admirers in A's territory. Photograph by Laurence Hyman.

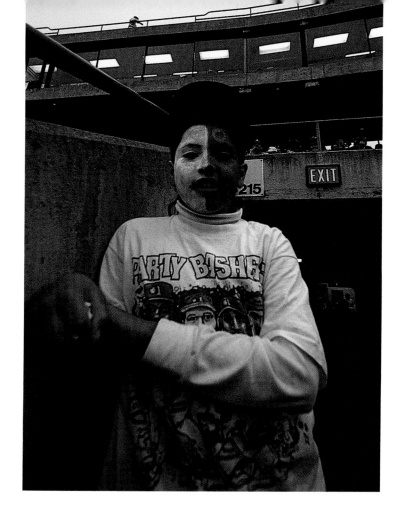

Will Clark and Mark
McGwire reserve their
rivalry for the game.
Photograph by Martha
Jane Stanton.

Dave Stewart and Giants hitting coach Dusty Baker, once Dodgers teammates, are reunited in the Series while former Giants teammates Dave Henderson and Robby Thompson get reacquainted. Photographs by Martha Jane Stanton. Brett Butler sends a message home. Photograph by Dennis Desprois. Opposite page, the same game, different worlds. Photograph by Martha Jane Stanton.

The third deck of the Coliseum affords a panoramic view of play. Participating in the World Series is as great an honor for umpires as it is for players. Photographs by Michael Zagaris. Opposite, the Giants stand at attention during opening ceremonies. Photograph by Dennis Desprois.

The Series gets underway. Photograph by Dennis Desprois. At times, the entire Bay Area seems tuned to the same frequency. Photograph by Michael Jang.

A Bay Series
at Last

by Bruce Jenkins

The afternoon of October 17, 1989, had a balmy, almost tropical feel at Candlestick Park. It was just about the best day imaginable for baseball. The Oakland Athletics had dominated the first two games of the World Series, but that wonderful sense of urgency filled the air. This was Game 3 of an all-Bay Area matchup, and the San Francisco Giants were about to play their first World Series home game in 27 years.

At 5:04 p.m., about a half-hour before game time, the Series—and the lives of countless Northern Californians—were forever altered. A massive earthquake, measured at 7.1 on the Richter scale, rocked the stadium. For a few horrifying seconds, as the upper deck trembled and the light towers swayed grotesquely from side to side, one got the feeling that Candlestick might crumble to the ground.

Somehow, it didn't. And the crowd, relieved of its shock and apprehension, began to cheer.

Within minutes, some rather nervous jokes were being told—in the stands, in the press box, and down on the field, where the pre-game warmups had been so rudely interrupted. "I guess the momentum has shifted," said Giants pitcher Atlee Hammaker, and one of the club executives was heard to remark, "Do we stage a pre-game show here, or what?"

Levity was the appropriate response at Candlestick, because there was so little sense of the tragedy outside. ABC television had lost its power, cutting off broadcaster Al Michaels in mid-sentence: "We're having an earth . . . " The game had been postponed, quickly and decisively, by Baseball Commissioner Fay Vincent. But it would be hours before the World Series crowd realized the full weight of this disaster. For those who drove into San Francisco that night, negotiating pitch-black neighborhoods that seemed only vaguely familiar, the crisis became abundantly clear.

The following day, after meeting with representatives of the teams and cities, Vincent held a press conference by candlelight at the St. Francis Hotel. It had been just two months since he had replaced A. Bartlett Giamatti, who died so suddenly of a heart attack, but now Vincent was the central figure in a predicament that called for sensitivity and tact. "Ours is a modest little game," said Vincent. "We're only guests here." And he postponed Game 3 until Tuesday, October 24, emphasizing that if the community wasn't ready by that date, then baseball wouldn't be ready, either.

In some ways, the World Series never recovered. Many out-of-town journalists, shocked and disillusioned, left San Francisco and did not return. A good number of fans lost their zest for the game. For the players, trying to stay sharp in intrasquad workouts, it was a time to reflect—on their profession, on the crisis at hand, and on the events leading up to it.

"It doesn't feel like a very important job right now," said Giants Manager Roger Craig. "But I'm trying to make sure these guys realize how far we've come this year—and why."

It had been an unforgettable season for both teams. The Giants, picked to finish third or fourth by most experts, took an undisputed hold on first place June 17 and never relinquished it, clinching the title on a dramatic night at Dodger Stadium, September 27. The Giants lost that game, 1-0, but after waiting around the clubhouse for more than an hour, they learned that the second-place San Diego Padres had lost in extra innings to Cincinnati. It was a moment of triumph for Craig, whose injury-plagued pitching staff nearly crumbled, and for

General Manager Al Rosen, who made the National League's most significant trade when he picked up reliever Steve Bedrosian from Philadelphia in mid-season.

In a fascinating coincidence, the A's clinched the American League West title that same night. And theirs had been an equally difficult road. No less than six key players—Jose Canseco, Mark McGwire, Dennis Eckersley, Bob Welch, Walt Weiss and Storm Davis—suffered major injuries before the All-Star break. Canseco didn't play at all until mid-July. "Somehow, we kept it all together," said Manager Tony La Russa, "and when we all got healthy, we could smell it."

There were banner individual seasons on both sides. A's third baseman Carney Lansford took a run at the batting title (.336), Dave Stewart notched his third consecutive 20-win season, Eckersley walked an incredible three batters in 57 2/3 innings, and Mike Moore—a timely purchase from the free-agent market—went 19-11. The Giants got an MVP season from Kevin Mitchell (47 homers), but teammate Will Clark nearly stole the trophy with his .333 average, 23 homers and 111 RBIs. Scott Garrelts edged the Dodgers' Orel Hershisher for the ERA title (2.28) and third baseman Matt Williams managed a remarkable 44 home runs in a season split between San Francisco and Phoenix.

Then came the playoffs—a one-week stretch that probably saw the all-time peak of professional baseball in the Bay Area. The A's dismantled Toronto in five games, featuring two wins from Dave Stewart, a tape-measure home run by Jose Canseco at the SkyDome (it was measured at 475 feet, but witnesses insisted on 550 or longer), and a fabulous all-around display by Rickey Henderson. Acquired from the Yankees in a mid-season trade, Henderson hit .400 with two home runs, seven walks, eight stolen bases and untold doses of intimidation, reaffirming the popular notion that he is the greatest leadoff man in history.

Longtime observers said they'd never seen a playoff performance quite like Henderson's. But that was before Will Clark got through with the Chicago Cubs. In the opener at Wrigley Field, Clark went 4-for-5 with a grand slam and six RBIs. In the climactic Game 5 at Candlestick, he tripled to set up the tying run in the seventh, then ripped a two-run, game-winning single in a riveting confrontation with reliever Mitch "Wild Thing" Williams in the eighth. Clark's gorgeous swing had already inspired comparisons to Stan Musial, Ted Williams and the great hitters of the past. In the wake of his playoff series—.650 average, 24 total bases—any comparison seemed valid. "Will Clark," said Giants catcher Terry Kennedy, "is the greatest baseball player I've ever seen."

There was only one drawback to the Giants' and A's playoff performances—they accomplished their missions too quickly. A full five days would pass before the World Series opened on Saturday, October 14, at the Oakland Coliseum. Something was lost that week, particularly on the Giants' side. Their swashbuckling, "Humm-Baby" brand of baseball never really surfaced again. But then, they were up against one of the greatest teams of the modern era.

Stewart turned Game 1 into his personal showcase. While the A's pecked away at Scott Garrelts, including solo homers by Dave Parker and Walt Weiss, Stewart crafted a masterpiece. This was a man who, despite those three 20-win seasons, had never won the Cy Young Award. Finishing this game, especially with a shutout, would be his crowning moment, and nobody understood that more than A's Manager Tony La Russa. Even in a ninth-inning crisis—two on, nobody out—La Russa bypassed Eckersley and stuck with his ace. The result was a crisp 5-0 victory, and when a triumphant Stewart walked off the field, the tone of this World Series was set.

By the end of Game 2, Craig faced a bitter irony. Moore went seven strong innings in a 5-1 victory, using the same split-fingered fastball that made Stewart so effective in the opener. That was Roger Craig's pitch, the one he taught so effectively to the Giants' pitchers over the years. Now he was being beaten by his own weapon.

Giants starter Rick Reuschel, meanwhile, had one of the worst outings of his life. Slipping completely out of character, he started out by walking Rickey Henderson on four pitches. "I can't remember him even throwing THREE straight balls," said pitching coach Norm Sherry. But the A's, as it turned out, had Reuschel's number.

"They had the reputation as first-ball hitters, but they waited me out tonight," said Reuschel. "They put me in a situation where I had to put the ball in there." Reuschel paid a heavy price, notably Terry Steinbach's three-run homer in the fourth inning. Another night, another convincing A's victory—and a bleak World Series future for the Giants.

"You can see how the A's have learned their lesson from last year, when they lost to the Dodgers," said Kennedy. "The experience obviously taught them something. They've got a real air of confidence about them." And while some of the Giants talked bravely, Kevin Mitchell was brutally candid. "I don't know why, but it's just not as exciting as it was in the playoffs," said Mitchell. "It's so calm. It seems like everybody's dead now."

Getting back to Candlestick, they surmised, would be just the ticket. Then came the earthquake, and life would never be quite the same.

To their everlasting credit, the Candlestick fans filed calmly and quietly out of the stadium after Game 3 had been postponed that night. "It was amazing," said Giants executive Corey Busch. "There could have been a stampede, complete panic, but the fans kept their cool. I'll never forget that."

Each of the players went through his own private hell. Gene Nelson was sitting in a corner of the clubhouse when the earthquake struck, "and all the concrete pillars were shaking," he said. "Dust was falling down. I was absolutely sure the stadium was going to come down on me." Tony Phillips felt like going home to Arizona immediately, a fear that took him days to shake. Pat Sheridan's wife had not yet arrived at Candlestick when the earthquake hit, and while he soon learned that she was fine, he never regained his interest in playing (in an Associated Press poll a few days after the quake, Sheridan was the only man on either team who wanted the Series cancelled). Bob Welch and his wife learned that their new home, a second-story condominium in the Marina district, had been badly damaged.

As the days went on, it became evident that a one-week delay wasn't long enough. Vincent, after conferring with the teams, San Francisco Mayor Art Agnos and the structural engineers examining Candlestick, decided that Game 3 would be played on Friday, October 27 – a 10-day layoff. And he met little opposition.

"Fay Vincent is a brilliant administrator of meetings," said A's General Manager Sandy Alderson. "He gave everyone their say. He obviously has a completely open mind. His judgments are the assimilation of everything he hears and thinks. Yet there is no question as to who is the Commissioner."

Neither team approached its workouts with much verve, but there was a significant difference. The A's looked upon the World Series as an opportunity. For the Giants, it was more of an obligation.

"Personally, I can take it or leave it," said Giants player representative Brett Butler. "If we play, we'll play to win. But to be honest, I just don't care."

Craig tried to loosen things up, saying he planned to manage the rest of the Series from second base, but hanging around Candlestick – which had now taken on a strange, eerie feel – made it difficult. Mitchell was openly depressed, saying, "I feel sort of bad all over, I don't know what it is. Maybe my body is telling me this is the time of the year to shut down." The Giants even had a freak injury when Reuschel, who was standing in the outfield during a workout, was struck in the shoulder by a line drive and forced out of the rotation.

Over at the Oakland Coliseum, the A's seemed a trifle uneasy, but mostly confident. They were the ones with the 2-0 lead, and La Russa seized an obvious advantage by naming Stewart and Moore as his starters for Games 3 and 4. They were going for the kill. They also had a nice change of scenery, moving to Phoenix for the final two days of preparation. They were surrounded by adoring fans in their intrasquad workouts. Suddenly, they felt important again. "One look at those fans, and the soreness in my legs was gone," said Mark McGwire.

In the grand, cosmic scheme of things, the Giants seemed destined to win Game 3. No other scenario would be appropriate; the Bay Area had waited too long for an A's-Giants World Series to have it disappear into oblivion. But it did – and Dave Stewart, the Oakland native, was a big reason why.

In the nights following the earthquake, Stewart found himself getting out of bed and driving to the gruesome scene at the Cypress section of I-880. "I don't even know why," he said. "There was something inside me that wasn't settled. I kept coming back and telling my friends, 'There are people still alive in there. I know it.'" Then, one miraculous day, Buck Helm emerged from the wreckage, and became the symbol of the Bay Area's recovery spirit. "Maybe that's what I needed to see," said Stewart.

When Stewart arrived at Candlestick Park that Friday night, he was focused and ready. That's more than one could say for many of the fans and players, but in a tasteful pre-game ceremony, the Giants eased some of the tension. They asked for a moment of silence at 5:04 p.m., then had the entire stadium singing along with members of the cast of "Beach Blanket Babylon" in a rendition of the 1936 Jeanette McDonald tune, "San Francisco." The first pitch was thrown out, collectively, by a dozen representatives of the earthquake relief effort.

And when the game started, it didn't take long to ignite. Garrelts threw a first-inning fastball near the head of Canseco, who took a few menacing steps toward the mound, and with a true sense of drama in the air, the fans found themselves enraptured by the game of baseball.

Unfortunately for the Giants, it was a little too much Oakland baseball. The A's had a 13-3 lead at one point, and only a late, futile rally made the score a more respectable 13-7. Dave Henderson hit two homers, and nearly missed a third when his off-field drive struck the top rail of the right-field fence. Canseco, breaking an 0-for-23 Series slump dating back to last year, had two singles and a homer. And Stewart, who would be voted MVP, pitched five-hit ball for seven innings.

"There's just a different feeling when Stewart walks out to pitch," said Steinbach. "He makes everyone feel good about himself." And that was a pretty good description of the crowd's late-inning mood, despite the distasteful score. In a new state of earthquake consciousness, many of the fans had come equipped with flashlights. As if on cue, a bank of lights went out in centerfield, and within minutes hundreds of flashlights were blinking in the upper deck, creating a wonderful, festive atmosphere. "I felt like I was at a Rolling Stones concert," said Will Clark. "It's like people were saying, 'We're just glad to be alive.' "

It wasn't until the latter stages of Game 4, on another beautiful night at Candlestick, that the '89 World Series came through as advertised. The A's took an 8-0 lead, looking postively awe-inspiring in the process, but the Giants came back to within 8-6. This was the essence of both teams, the fiber on which their seasons were built. And now Will Clark was at the plate, facing Rick Honeycutt in the seventh inning, with a chance to tie the game with a home run.

Clark got a slider—"a pitch I'll see all winter long," he said—and popped it up for the second out. Then came Mitchell, whose two-run homer in the sixth had ended Moore's shutout bid. He sent a deep drive toward left, but with a little something missing. "The first ball left his bat like a rocket," said Phillips. "This one looked more like a changeup." When Rickey Henderson caught the ball on the warning track, the Giants' last real opportunity had expired.

The A's had some vintage moments, including Henderson's game-opening home run and a shocking, two-run double by Moore. Not only had Moore batted just once in his career, American League pitchers were 0-for-70 in the World Series dating back to 1979. "When I saw that, I realized that the A's were a tidal wave," said Kennedy. "And there was nothing we could do to stop it."

The game drew another lively, energetic group of fans, 62,000 strong, and they were treated to a spectacularly fine moment in the eighth inning when Clark, in pursuit of a foul ball, flipped over the shallow railing in front of the field boxes and landed directly in Vincent's lap. "I saw Clark coming out of the corner of my eye," said the Commissioner with a smile. "But I had that ball all the way."

Fittingly, for those who truly appreciated the A's talent, the Series ended with pitching and defense. Eckersley needed just four pitches to record three outs, and Phillips made back-to-back sensational plays at second base. His game-ending flip to Eckersley, adroitly covering first on Butler's grounder to the right side, was a testament to fundamental baseball. "And that," said La Russa, "is what the A's are all about."

There was no champagne in the A's clubhouse. After all that had happened in Northern California, this was no time for childish slapstick. But the A's had a classy, dignified little celebration, and the Giants felt surprisingly good themselves. "When you're beaten that convincingly," said Craig, "you have to tip your hat. We're just glad to have played in the World Series. That's what we'll take home with us."

When people look back on the 1989 World Series, they'll find it one of the most lopsided ever played. But it will take a singular position in the history books, because there was no precedent for what the Giants and A's were asked to do. In that sense, it was unforgettable. And in the end, there were no losers.

Oakland ace Dave Stewart
overpowers the Giants in
Game 1. A's second baseman
Tony Phillips tags a sliding
Brett Butler. Photographs by
Michael Zagaris.

Scott Garrelts leaves
the game after Oakland
scores five runs
through four innings.
The A's contain
the power of Matt
Williams. Opposite
page, Terry Kennedy
attempts to break up
the double play as
shortstop Walt Weiss
fires the ball to first.
Photographs by
Dennis Desprois.
Kennedy's second
inning catching error
allows Terry Steinbach
to score. Photograph
by Michael Zagaris.

The MVPs of their respective playoff series, Will Clark and Rickey Henderson. Photographs by (top) Martha Jane Stanton and (right) Michael Zagaris.

A picture-perfect Mark McGwire swing
results in a broken bat; Matt Williams
retrieves the barrel. Veteran Dave Parker
relishes his Game 1 homer. Photographs by Michael Zagaris.

Roger Craig signals to the bull-pen for relief. Photograph by Dennis Desprois. Dave Henderson greets Terry Steinbach with a bash. Photograph by Roy Garibaldi. Opposite, Oakland fans exult in their first victory. Photograph by Michael Jang. A's announcer Bill King talks shop with Hank Greenwald, voice of the Giants. Photograph by Martha Jane Stanton.

A's faithful can only hope the Giants find Mike Moore's pitching bewitching. Photograph by Michael Zagaris. Ingenuity knows no bounds during the Series. Photograph by Martha Jane Stanton.

Opposite, Mike Moore holds the Giants to a single run in Game 2. Photograph by Michael Zagaris. Matt Williams tags out would-be base thief Rickey Henderson. Photograph by Roy Garibaldi.

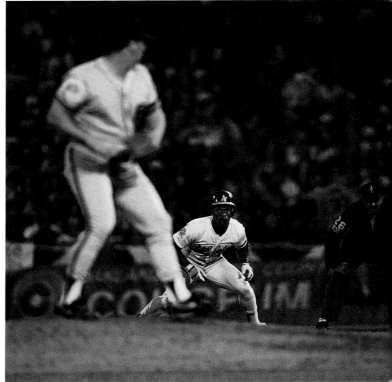

Mark McGwire smacks a double off Game 2 reliever Kelly Downs. Photograph by Michael Zagaris.

Rick Reuschel faces the consequences of allowing Rickey
Henderson to reach base. Photographs by Michael Zagaris.
A frustrated Roger Craig searches for a chink in the A's
armor. Photograph by Dennis Desprois.

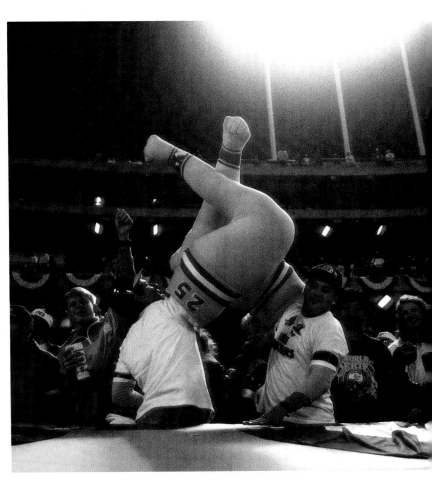

Clockwise from left: Rick Reuschel gets knocked out in the fifth inning.
Photograph by Martha Jane Stanton. Kevin Mitchell raps a single in Game 2.
Reliever Dennis Eckersley closes the game. Photographs by Michael Zagaris.
Terry Steinbach's homer prompts a big bash in the stands. Photograph by Tak
Kuno. The results of Games 1 and 2 pop up in odd places.
Photograph by Michael Jang.

During the World Series, the Goodyear
Blimp is piloted by Tom Matus, who is pull-
ing for the A's, and Giants fan Charles Russell.
Photographs by Beth Hansen.

When you root for both teams, victory is always at hand. Photograph by Jon Winet. Candlestick Park draws its share of celebrities for Game 3, including Godzilla and the Montanas. Photographs by Michael Jang.

An unusually mild
October puts pre-
game revelers and the
Giants band in an
exceptionally festive
mood. Photographs
on this page by (top)
Michael Jang, (bottom)
Jon Winet. Opposite
page photographs by
Beth Hansen.

Many cars in the Candlestick parking lot bear evidence of intense team loyalty. Photograph by Jon Winet. A couple of A's fans brave a crowd of Giants rooters. Photograph by Michael Jang. Opposite page, Game 3 tickets will soon become collector's items. Rick Reuschel's fans stand by their man. Photographs by Jon Winet.

In the quiet hours before the game, players start workouts while Giants Owner Bob Lurie and President and GM Al Rosen delight in returning to their home turf for the third contest of the Series. Photograph by Dennis Desprois. Photograph (top) by Beth Hansen.

The pre-game ballpark is a mecca for young autograph seekers. Photograph by Martha Jane Stanton. Jose Canseco bears the brunt of one fan's ribbing. Photograph by Michael Zagaris. The two managers await the start of the game that never happened. Photograph by Dennis Desprois.

Prior to Game 3, a friendship withstands the tug of team loyalties, Giants fans get into the spirit of the season, artist LeRoy Neiman and infielder Chris Speier capture the scene, and A's players appear eager to get the game underway. Photographs by (counter-clockwise from left) Brad Chaney, Martha Jane Stanton, Michael Zagaris, Martha Jane Stanton, Michael Zagaris.

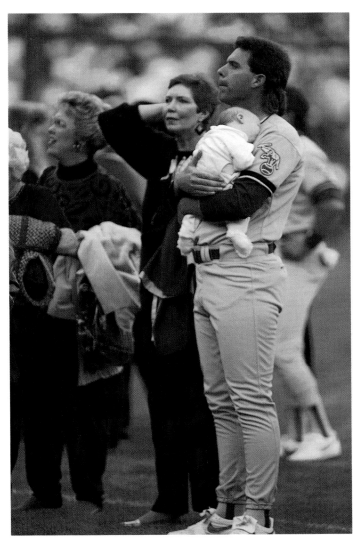

At 5:04 the stadium is rocked for 15 seconds by the Bay Area's strongest earthquake since 1906. Storm Davis and other players are reunited with their families on the field after the scoreboard and stadium lights are knocked out. Baseball Commissioner Fay Vincent and staff express shock. Team executives Pat Gallagher and Sandy Alderson confer while manager Roger Craig scans the stands. Photographs by (clockwise from bottom) Dennis Desprois, Michael Zagaris, Dennis Desprois, Bodie Hyman, Martha Jane Stanton.

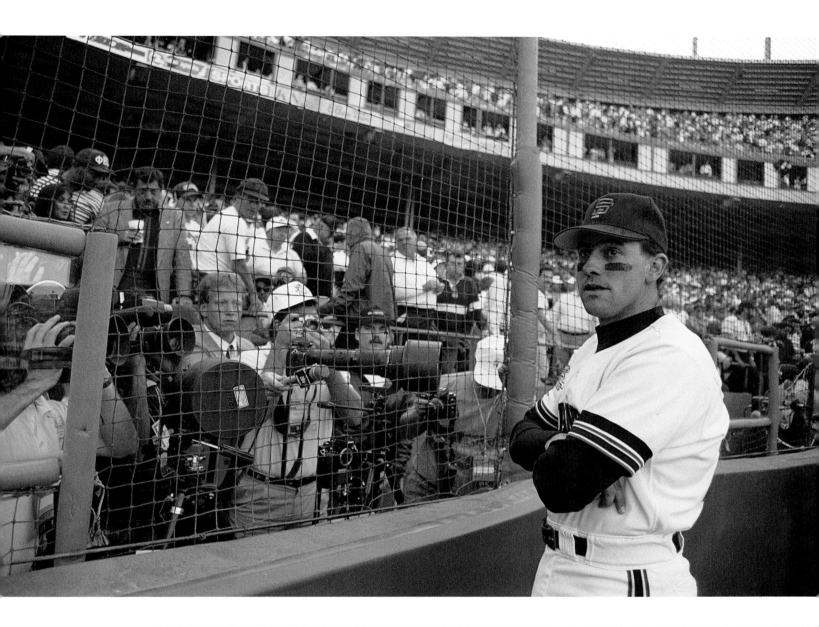

Opposite, Police Chief
Frank Jordan takes
charge. Photograph
by Dennis Desprois.
A's players help their
families out of the
stands. Photograph
by Martha Jane Stanton.
Will Clark waits for
his father (in red
shirt) to join him on
the field. Photograph
by Martha Jane Stanton.
Kevin Mitchell and
Willie Mays anxiously
survey the stadium.
Photograph by Otto
Greule, Jr./Allsport USA.

After 20 minutes and several aftershocks, fans file out of Candlestick and begin to realize the extent of the earthquake damage. Photographs by (top) Jon Winet and (bottom) Martha Jane Stanton.

Many players, including Giants pitcher Kelly Downs, don't take time to change out of uniform before leaving Candlestick with their families. Photograph by Cynthia Kane. A plume of smoke rising from San Francisco's shattered Marina District is the first sign for many of the quake's catastrophic effects. Photograph by Bodie Hyman.

The Bay Area immediately shifts its attention from World Series play to the 7.1 earthquake that cripples the Bay Bridge and ravages San Francisco's Marina District. Photograph (right) by Michael Jang. Other photographs by Debora Cartwright.

Brick buildings, such as one at Sixth and Townsend Streets in San Francisco, and many structures built on landfill, are hardest hit. Photographs by (clockwise from left) Michael Jang, Brad Chaney, Mari Kane, David Lilienstein, Roy Garibaldi, Brad Chaney.

Rescue crews labor for days to free those trapped in Oakland's collapsed I-880 freeway. Photographs by (clockwise from top) Roy Shigley, Roy Garibaldi, Michael Jang.

Cracks wind through the streets of San Francisco. Photograph by Jon Winet. After extinguishing Marina District fires, crews assess damage. Photograph by Mari Kane.

Amazingly, a lone section of Oakland's Cypress structure remains intact. Photograph by Roy Shigley. CBS anchorman Dan Rather broadcasts from an improvised set near the scene. Photograph by Roy Garibaldi. Opposite, San Francisco's most heavily damaged areas are cordoned off while awaiting inspection. Photographs by (top) Otto Greule, Jr./Allsport USA and (bottom) Mari Kane.

Marina District neighbors are reunited as they line up at a relief center. Photograph by Michael Jang. Union Square merchants such as I. Magnin scramble to repair damage and reopen their doors. Photograph by David Lilienstein.

Opposite, the process of rebuilding begins with more destruction. Photograph (far right) by Mari Kane. Other photographs by Brad Chaney.

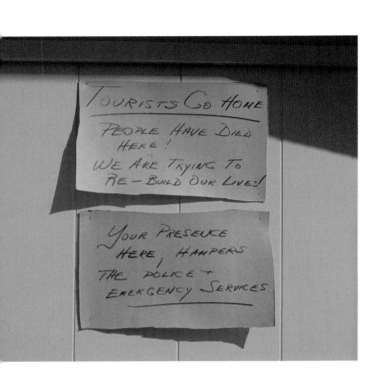

Opposite, beleaguered Marina residents quickly grow weary of sightseers flocking to their neighborhood. Photograph by Jon Winet. Most San Francisco businesses escape the kind of major structural damage that devastated the largely residential Marina. Photographs by (top right) Mari Kane and (bottom) Roy Shigley. Although it survived the 1906 earthquake, the Golden Gate Park band shell portico sustains severe damage during the October 17 quake. Photograph by Cynthia Kane. Photograph (right) by Jon Winet.

Entrepreneurs quickly expand their line of World Series memorabilia. Photograph by Laurence Hyman. The dismantling of I-880 begins. Photograph by Roy Shigley. Opposite page, San Francisco's historic Geary Theatre sustains massive damage just hours before a scheduled performance. Photograph by Frederic Larson, courtesy of the San Francisco Chronicle. Two days after the quake, newspapers document the growing sense of recovery. Photograph by Michael Jang.

By night, the lack of headlights on the Bay Bridge is the only clue that anything is amiss in San Francisco. Photograph by Laurence Hyman.

Makeshift T-shirt stands spring up across Northern California. Photograph by Michael Jang. Despite set-backs caused by the earthquake, merchants carry on with business. Photograph by Cynthia Kane. Opposite, with the Bay Bridge down, ferries become a vital link across the Bay for thousands of commuters. Photographs by Roy Shigley.

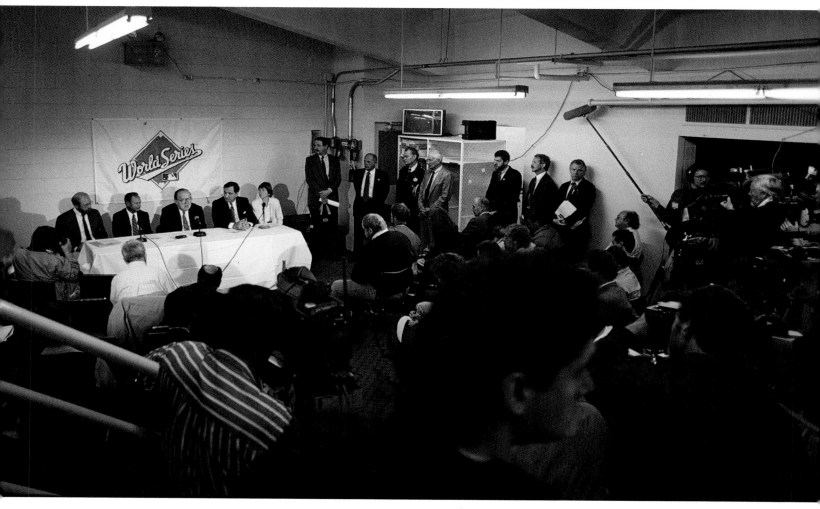

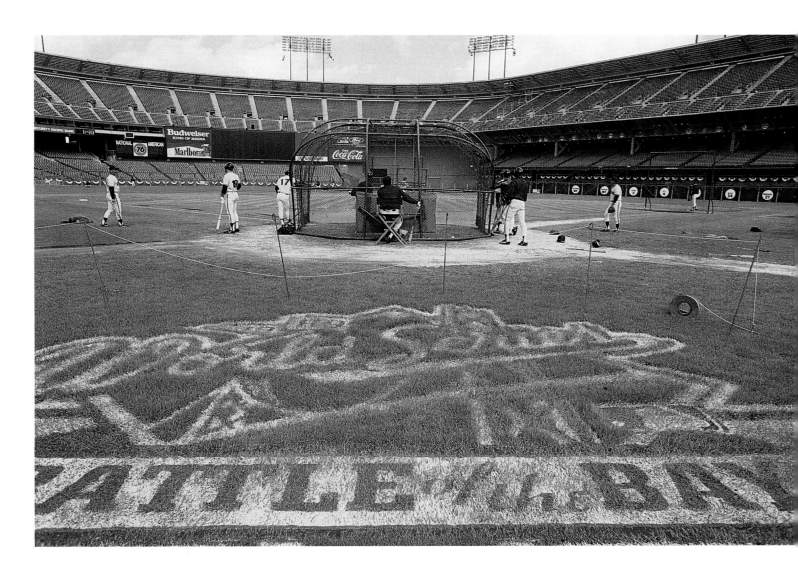

Once the stadium is deemed structurally sound, Bob
Brenly and the Giants resume workouts, but a decidedly
somber air pervades Candlestick. Baseball Commissioner
Fay Vincent holds a press conference with Oakland
Mayor Lionel Wilson and San Francisco Mayor Art Agnos
to announce baseball's role in earthquake relief. Photo-
graphs by (clockwise from left) Dennis Desprois,
Dennis Desprois, Jon Winet, Dennis Desprois, Martha
Jane Stanton.

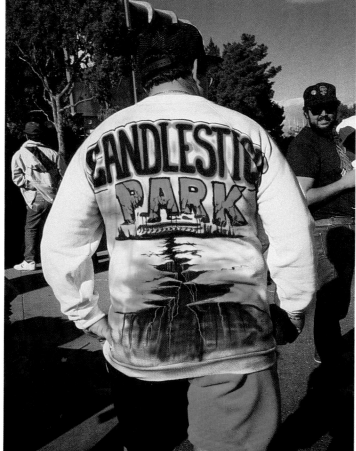

The earthquake still looms large in the minds of fans who gather once again at Candlestick for Game 3. Photographs by (clockwise from left) Jon Winet, Michael Jang, Michael Zagaris, Jon Winet.

Opposite, Baseball Commissioner Fay Vincent and wife Valerie return to Candlestick for Game 3. Photograph by Laurence Hyman. Rickey Henderson talks with Dave Stewart, who is able to start Game 3 because of the earthquake delay. Superstar Rickey Henderson strolls past baseball legend Joe DiMaggio, seated in the VIP field box. Photographs by Michael Zagaris. Hall of Famer Willie Mays eases tension in the Giants dugout. Photograph by Dennis Desprois.

On the preceding page: With the Bay Area on the road to recovery, fans return to Candlestick on October 27 for Game 3 of the Series. Photograph by Robert La Mar. Above, fans observe a moment of silence at 5:04 for victims of the quake. Photograph by Bodie Hyman. Cast members of "Beach Blanket Babylon" lead the crowd in the singing of "San Francisco." Photograph by Michael Zagaris. Opposite page, the blimp returns to Candlestick after being called into service for media coverage of the earthquake. Twelve heroes of the relief effort throw out the first balls of Game 3. Photographs by Beth Hansen.

In their second attempt to get Game 3 under way, managers and umpires hope for no unexpected disruptions. Photograph by Dennis Desprois. Although not included on the post-season roster, veteran Giants catcher Bob Brenly remains a supportive member of the team throughout the Series. Photograph by Martha Jane Stanton. Opposite, shadows envelop Candlestick soon after the game starts. Photograph by Roy Shigley.

Jose Canseco takes exception to a razor-close Scott Garrelts pitch in the early going. Leadoff hitter Brett Butler lays down a bunt. Photographs by Martha Jane Stanton. Opposite, it takes a headfirst slide for Rickey Henderson to beat third base-man Ken Oberkfell's tag. Photograph by Dennis Desprois. A sizzling Dave Henderson goes 3-for-4 with a pair of homers. Photograph by Michael Zagaris.

Bill Bathe's pinch-hit home run fuels a ninth-inning Giants rally. Photograph by Michael Zagaris. The dark clouds hovering over Candlestick seem to portend disappointment for anxious Giants fans. Photograph (right) by Roy Garibaldi. Other photographs by Beth Hansen.

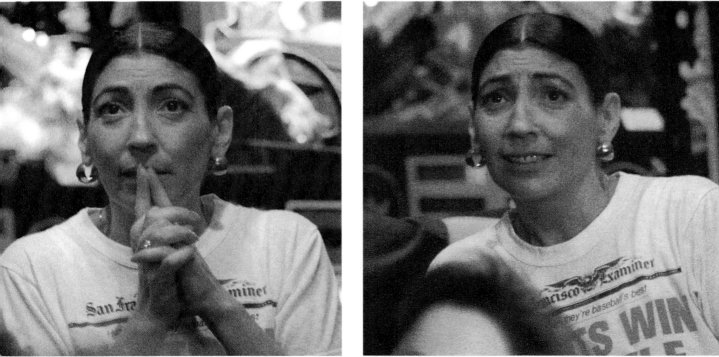

Jose Canseco blasts a three-run homer in Game 3, then receives a bash from teammates Carney Lansford and Rickey Henderson. Photographs by Michael Zagaris. Oakland fans thrill to their team's success. Photograph by Beth Hansen.

Shortstop Jose Uribe contemplates the Herculean task that lies ahead for his team, down 3-0 in the Series. Photograph by Martha Jane Stanton. A's boosters couldn't be happier with their team's prospects. Photograph by Beth Hansen. Opposite, Kevin Mitchell stops by the field box seats of National League President Bill White and Giants great Willie Mays. Photograph by Michael Zagaris. Vendors of World Series memorabilia do a brisk business. Photograph by Beth Hansen.

121

A's Stan Javier, Dave Parker, and Rickey
Henderson stay loose before the game. Photograph by Michael Zagaris. A couple of scary-
looking fans get a dubious look from comedian
Will Durst. Photograph by Dennis Desprois.

Baseball fans of all ages relish the World Series experience. Photographs by Martha Jane Stanton. Pitchers Dennis Eckersley and Bob Welch wait in the visitor's clubhouse. Photograph by Michael Zagaris.

A's outfielder Dave Henderson clowns
with National Anthem singer Nell Carter.
Photograph by Roy Garibaldi. Candlestick turns chilly as clouds roll over
the stadium. Photograph by Beth Hansen.

Despite a painful knee condition, Don Robinson starts Game 4. Photograph by Dennis Desprois. Rickey Henderson launches the third pitch of the game beyond the left field fence. Photograph by Martha Jane Stanton.

Third base coach Rene Lachemann congratulates Rickey Henderson. Manager Roger Craig yanks a frustrated Don Robinson in the second inning with the Giants down 4-0. Photographs by Martha Jane Stanton.

Kevin Mitchell is greeted by third base coach Bill Fahey after his two-run homer puts the Giants on the board. Photograph by Dennis Desprois. Brett Butler takes out A's second baseman Tony Phillips to break up the double play. Photograph by Michael Zagaris.

Will Clark deprives Baseball
Commissioner Fay Vincent of a
souvenir by going the extra
mile for a foul ball. Photographs
by Dennis Desprois.

Denied his designated hitter role in the National League park, Dave Parker pinch hits for pitcher Todd Burns in Game 4. Photograph by Michael Zagaris. It's all over and the Oakland Athletics are on top of the world. Photograph by Dennis Desprois.

Opposite, an Oakland team that was denied the World Series title a year earlier rejoices in its decisive 1989 victory. Photograph by Michael Zagaris. Fans spill into the streets of Oakland to celebrate their championship. Mark McGwire and his fiancée, Ame Blackshear, let the headlines speak for themselves. Photographs (top and right) by Roy Shigley. Photograph (above) by Roy Garibaldi.

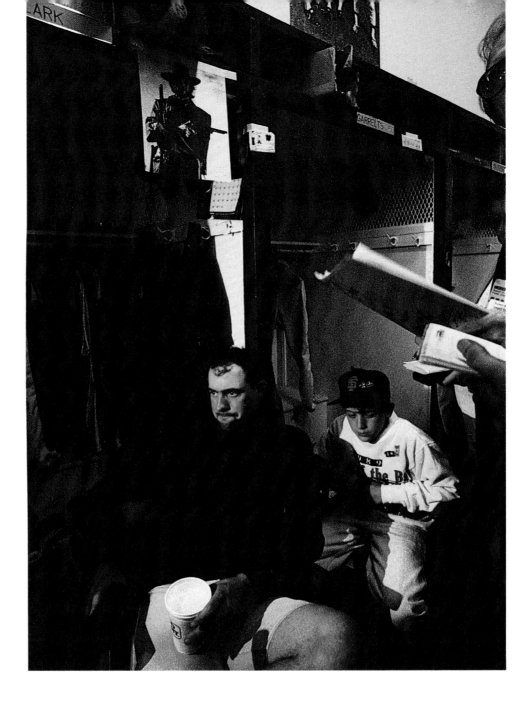

Opposite, an A's fan revels in the Series sweep, but defeat is difficult to swallow for a young Giants rooter. Photographs by (top) Roy Shigley and (bottom) Beth Hansen. Will Clark and his younger brother, Scott, share disappointment in the Giants clubhouse. Photograph by Laurence Hyman. In the streets of Oakland, a party atmosphere takes hold. Photograph by Roy Shigley.

A's players, including Dave Parker, gather later in the evening to relive highlights of the Series. Photograph by Beth Hansen. Photograph (below) by Roy Shigley. Opposite, Dave Henderson savors the championship. Photograph by Michael Zagaris.

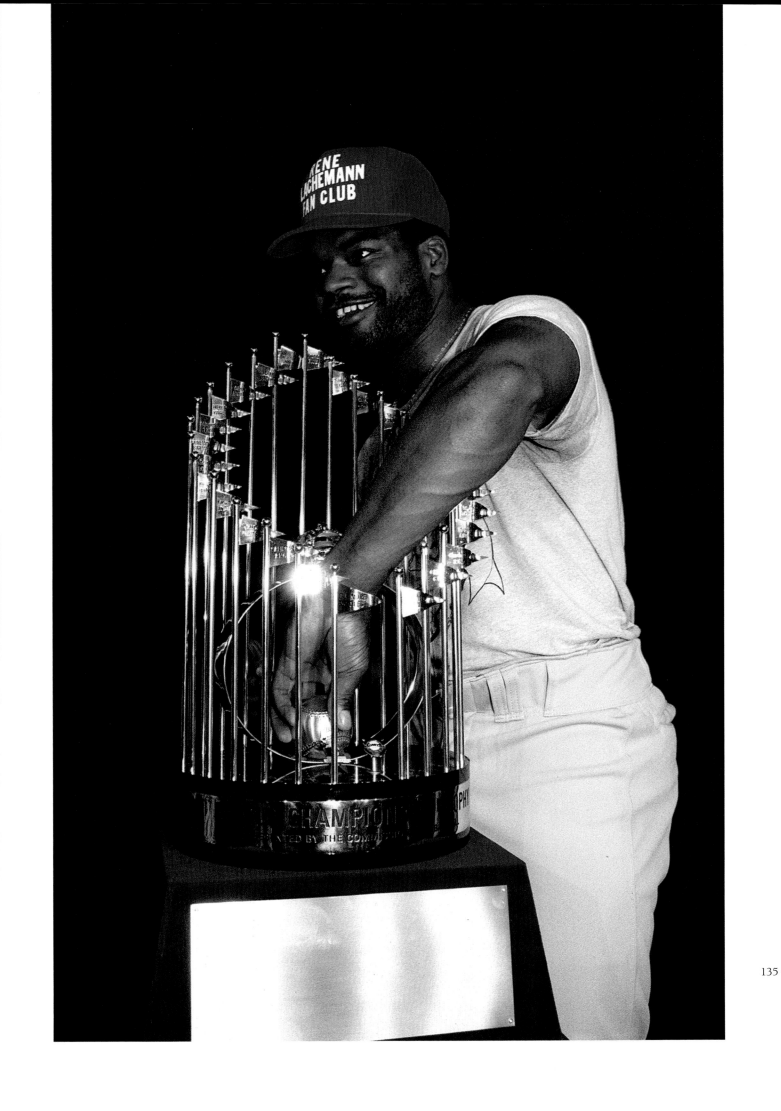

Oakland faithful flock to Jack London Square to cheer for their heroes at the championship rally. Photographs by Roy Shigley.

Dave Stewart, Rickey Henderson, and the rest of the
A's arrive by ferry at the Jack London Square
celebration. Photographs by (top) Roy Garibaldi
and (bottom) Roy Shigley.

Oakland manager Tony La Russa accepts the community's congratulations as A's Owner and Managing General Partner Walter A. Haas, Jr. and Oakland Mayor Lionel Wilson proudly look on. Photographs by Roy Garibaldi. Dave Henderson and his son bask in the glow of victory with Series MVP Dave Stewart. Photograph by Roy Shigley.

One week after World Series regalia comes down in Candle-stick, San Francisco voters reject the ballpark initiative. For Giants utility infielder Chris Speier, the Series caps the final season of his nineteen-year big league career. Photographs by Dennis Desprois.

A partisan Bay Bridge
toll taker delights in
backing a winner. Pho-
tograph by Roy Shigley.
At Ocean Beach, a
young Giants fan con-
tinues to wear his
team's colors. Photo-
graph by Michael Jang.

The banners are gone, the rallies are over, but memories of a first-ever cross-Bay Series—and the earthquake that shoved it from the front page—will not be forgotten by those who lived through these historic times. Photographs by (above) Martha Jane Stanton and (right) Michael Jang. Photograph on following page by Brad Chaney.